POSSIBILITY THINKING

Given to _____

On this _____ day of _____

By _____

With this special message . . .

_____

_____

_____

POSSIBILITY THINKING

Inspiration from
Robert H. Schuller

THOMAS NELSON
PUBLISHERS

Published in Nashville, Tennessee by
Thomas Nelson Publishers.

**Library of Congress
Cataloging-in-Publication Data**

Schuller, Robert Harold.
    Possibility Thinking / Robert H.
Schuller.
        p.   cm. — (Itty Bitty book)
    ISBN 0-8407-6311-5 (TR)
    ISBN 0-7852-8264-5 (MM)
    1. Christian life—1960—Quotations,
maxims, etc.   2. Faith—Quotations,
maxims, etc.   I. Title   II. Series.
BV4905.2.S36   1993
242—dc20   93-20166
                                      CIP

Printed in Hong Kong
1 2 3 4 5 6 7 — 98 97 96 95 94 93

POSSIBILITY THINKING

Believe that for every problem, God will provide a solution.

———

LOVE IS THE POWER BEHIND FAITH.

Faith . . . is that mysterious something that turns an average person into an outstanding individual.

For every mountain, there's a miracle.

What appears to be the end of the road may just be a bend in the road . . . so don't slam on those <u>brakes</u>!

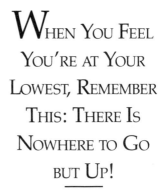

WHEN YOU FEEL YOU'RE AT YOUR LOWEST, REMEMBER THIS: THERE IS NOWHERE TO GO BUT UP!

When all else fails,
look for God's mercy.

HOPE-FILLED THINKING PRODUCES GREAT ENTHUSIASM!

Don't trust the clouds . . . trust the sunshine!

FAITH WITHOUT RISK IS A CONTRADICTION.

A believing love
takes away the weights
of doubt and gives
you wings of faith.

Have Faith in Your Faith ... Doubt Your Doubts.

Through faith,
weak times become
peak times.
___

F<small>AITH</small> . . . D<small>ON'T</small> B<small>LOCK</small> I<small>T</small> . . . U<small>NLOCK</small> I<small>T</small>!

Believe it and you will achieve it!

ALWAYS LOOK FOR THE POTENTIAL IN TODAY AND THE BEAUTY IN TOMORROW.

It costs nothing to
buy a dream . . .
and it's the best
investment you
can make.

SHAPE YOUR DREAMS BY YOUR HOPES, NOT BY YOUR HURTS.

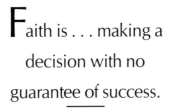

Faith is . . . making a decision with no guarantee of success.

Hope is its own immediate reward.

Hope is not the absence of suffering, it is living in the presence of love.

KEEP YOUR HEART RIGHT AND YOUR FAITH WILL BURN BRIGHT.

Prayer is the power that pulls everything together successfully.

Faith

Believes in
That Which
Can Never Be
Proven.

God does not see
you as what you are
but as what you
can become.

I Would Rather Err on the Side of Faith Than on the Side of Doubt.

No person is too small for God's love, and with that kind of love, no peak is too high to climb.

GOD
PROMISES
MERCY
ADEQUATE
ENOUGH TO
MEET ANY
TRAGEDY.

Possibility thinkers are incurably obsessed with the creative notion that the best is yet to be.

EVERYONE
NEEDS . . . A
PURPOSE TO LIVE
FOR . . . A SELF
THEY CAN LIVE
WITH . . . AND A
FAITH THEY CAN
LIVE BY.

Every Tomorrow Is a New Invitation to Beautiful Possibilities.

B e inspired by
God's nature: storms
always lose to the sun
. . . The sunrise always
overtakes the night . . .
And the winter always
turns into spring.

When faced with a mountain—I WILL NOT QUIT!

Surrender
Leadership to Only
One Thing . . .
Faith.

Don't be a fear thinker, be a faith thinker.

Nothing is too great for the God who gives impossible dreams.

Faith is . . . leaping the fence of limitations.

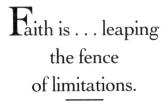

IF GOD BELIEVES IN YOU—YOU CAN TOO!

Faith is the force that
sets you free to
succeed.

Faith is Spelled, R-I-S-K!

Keep hope alive by tapping into the limitless power of prayer.

It takes but one positive thought, when given a chance to survive and thrive, to overpower an entire army of negative thoughts.

L<small>ET</small> G<small>O</small>
AND
L<small>ET</small> G<small>OD</small>.

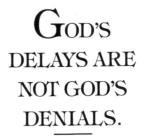

GOD'S DELAYS ARE NOT GOD'S DENIALS.

You must take the leap of faith to experience God's saving strength!

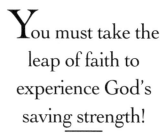

I WILL FACE MY FUTURE WITH FAITH, FOR I HAVE GOD BESIDE ME!

Thank God always.
Deep in the heart of
gratitude is a gift of
tremendous faith.

GOD IS PRESENT WITH YOU, IN SPITE OF WHAT THE CIRCUMSTANCES MIGHT APPEAR TO SAY.

Decide To Do Something Positive Today, and You Will Mount Up on Wings of Faith!

A strong faith is built on the joy of the Lord, and where there is joy, there is room only for the positive things in life!

Your life is in the
care and keeping of
God who keeps watch
over His own.

Faith
STIMULATES
SUCCESS.

Striving for excellence is an act of faith. God is not honored or glorified by mediocrity.

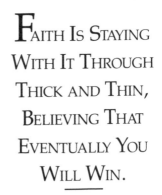

FAITH IS STAYING
WITH IT THROUGH
THICK AND THIN,
BELIEVING THAT
EVENTUALLY YOU
WILL WIN.

God does promise
He will bless us if we
are genuinely creative
and keep moving
ahead in faith.

GOD HAS PROMISED THAT HE WILL REWARD THE GOOD WORKER.

Keep the faith . . .
keep looking ahead!

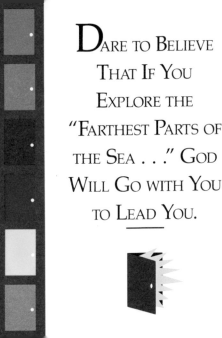

Dare to Believe That If You Explore the "Farthest Parts of the Sea . . ." God Will Go with You to Lead You.

We are guided not by sight, but insight—an innermost conscience that we believers call "faith."

GOD IS ABLE TO HEAL IF WE ARE ABLE TO BELIEVE!

Happy are the believers, for they need never worry!

CHOOSE FAITH OVER DOUBT. TO LIVE BY FAITH, ALL YOU HAVE TO DO IS CHOOSE IT. SUDDENLY, THE WAY BECOMES CLEAR.

Become a "do it now" person. The world is out there waiting to follow those who have faith to move ahead.

FAITH FINDS
ITS LIFE BY
SCANNING THE
HORIZON,
KNOWING
THERE WILL
BE A SUNRISE
TOMORROW.

To Live Is to Grow. Living by Faith Is Living the Healthy and Natural Way.

I am confident that: If there's a will, there's a way. If it's God's will, He will show the way. If I keep the faith, He will show me how!

HOPE

SUSTAINS

SUCCESS.

Look at your tears and build pillars of courageous faith into <u>your</u> life.

KEEP ON KEEPING ON. IT TAKES COURAGE, IT TAKES BOLDNESS, IT TAKES INTEGRITY.

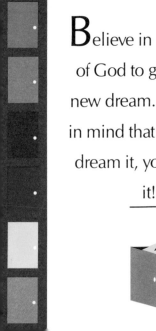

Believe in the power of God to give you a new dream. And bear in mind that if you can dream it, you can do it!

NEVER QUIT.
ALL YOU NEED
IS PATIENCE
THAT WILL
NEVER RUN
DRY.

Never

forget—there is a
light behind every
shadow. There can
be no shadow
unless a light is
shining somewhere.

Accept God's
forgiveness or you'll
treat yourself unfairly.

DON'T QUIT.
DON'T SPLIT. JUST
SIT. WAIT. GOD
WILL OUTLIVE,
OUTLAST, AND
OUTPERFORM YOUR
OPPONENT.

A Blind Man Sees with His Heart.

If a
disappointment
causes you to slip,
stumble, and
slide back into
discouragement,
then lift your mood
back up by giving
thanks to God
for all things.

People everywhere are the same. We share universal needs—the need for faith, hope, and love.

Love
SANCTIFIES
SUCCESS.

There are vast untapped resources of faith and talent that can be discovered only in adversity.

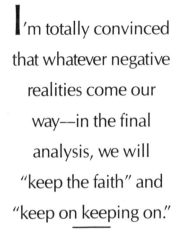

I'm totally convinced that whatever negative realities come our way—in the final analysis, we will "keep the faith" and "keep on keeping on."

Positive Prayer Starts with Two Life-Changing Words—"I Believe!"

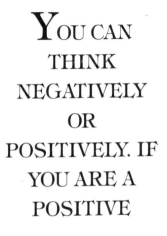

YOU CAN
THINK
NEGATIVELY
OR
POSITIVELY. IF
YOU ARE A
POSITIVE

THINKER, YOU
WILL BASE
YOUR
DECISIONS ON
FAITH, RATHER
THAN FEAR.

God is good! His spirit moves through the positive thinking mind and, instead of discouragement, there's a spirit of hope—of peace! Of new challenges!

Remember, you are surviving. You have a plan and you're working on it so that your dream will come true!

WHEN YOU THINK YOU HAVE EXHAUSTED ALL POSSIBILITIES, REMEMBER THIS . . . YOU HAVEN'T.

FORGIVENESS
IS WHERE WE
ENCOUNTER
GOD'S
GOODNESS . . .
FACE TO
FACE . . . HEART
TO HEART . . .

Positive feelings
always return! They
will inevitably come
to put sunshine back
into our lives!